ISBN: 978 09912402 – 8 - 9

i

Toni Cowart is a southern author and speaker who is passionate about sharing Jesus, hope and the peace that only He can give.

Toni's passion for helping others was ignited by her own personal experiences. Her history is sprinkled with tragedy and heartbreak, but her darkest moment is what most would call a parent's worst nightmare ~ burying three of her five children after a horrific car crash when a drunk driver crossed the center yellow line of a rural Alabama highway, turning her world upside down.

She speaks and writes through personal experiences from her darkest moments to her most joyous and peace filled life ~ life more abundant. It is her strong desire for others to know that they are not alone in their struggles nor through the dark journeys that life all too often drops in their paths.

Toni lives in North Alabama with her husband Chris. When she is not digging into God's Word, writing or speaking, she enjoys backyard gardening where her Bernedoodle Evie likes to "help".

IMPORTANT NOTE

**Please note: In this book, it is on purpose that the words:
satan, enemy, evil one, master manipulator or any other words used
to refer to "the thief" who comes to steal, kill and destroy,
are not capitalized. I will not give him upper case value.*

~ *A little more about me* ~

I would like to take this time, before we move into our study, to share why both Jesus and this study are so very precious to me.

I did not grow up in a Christian home. Sure, occasionally we went to church but that was few and far between. I did believe there was a God but did not know anything about the One they call Jesus.

I was grown, married and pregnant with my second child when I began to have this urge to attend a local church. I was searching for something but had no idea what. This would be a big deal for me to go to this church because my husband did not want to go when I asked him.

So, there I was, pregnant, a toddler on my hip and for this shy girl, it took a lot of mustering up of courage and that did not come natural for me. Off I went, a little scared of the unknown.

To my thankful heart, I was welcomed in a way that I had never known anywhere in my life. It was amazing. Someone invited me to Sunday School for the next week and I readily said yes even though I had no idea what to expect, but now I was eager.

You have to remember, not being raised in a Christian/church home, all the lingo and customs were so unfamiliar, but I felt embraced and welcomed and I was excited to go back the next week, and the next, and the next. I was quite eager and over the next few months something began to happen.

Something beautiful happened indeed. I found my Lord and Savior, Jesus Christ and accepted Him into my life. I had no idea just how much down the road I would need Him and His peace and strength.

As a brand, spanking new Christian I was mighty naive where church things were concerned. I found out that once you belong to Jesus and have been sealed as His – He begins to give you "heart smarts" and the things He places in your heart are much more valuable than any head knowledge one can have.

During the course of the next few weeks as I would go about my normal business, people from church would stop me and tell me how glad they were that I had joined their church or that I was now a member. I would just smile and not my head but I was a little confused.

You see, I was glad to be a part of their church but being a member of "such and such" church had nothing to do with why I walked down the isle that day. It was ALL about Jesus and this insatiable need I had for a Savior and a need that I really did not even understand. I had realized I needed a Savior and I did not want to go another minute, second or breath without Him.

I do know that it was divine intervention which led me to that particular church, the Spirit led Pastor, and the beautiful people who went on to mentor and disciple me.

My naivety was a blessing I believe. I was so hungry to know more about this Jesus; the One who forgives and I wanted to know all I could. I was not raised with all the Bible stories and the things that so many in our Bible belt are. So, I dug in and began to devour every bit of God's Word that I could.

I was ignorant enough to not know that so many Christians (Complacent or just following in someone else's footprints and not really having a personal relationship with Jesus) only pick up their Bible on Sunday, or on Easter or Christmas. I didn't know and so, little ol' me dug in and could not get enough. I still can't get enough and I don't ever want to get enough until I see my Jesus face to face.

I did not understand that during the time I was digging in and pouring over the scriptures, that my Lord was pouring back into me. I didn't know that what I held in my hands every time I was holding the Bible and reading His Word, that it was alive and active. I did not know I held a weapon and I did not know that He was preparing me. Preparing me for what was to come.

Fast forward, a few more children and many toils ~ God blessed me with five children and I had all five within nine years.

In spite of some dark things going on in my marriage, I thought I had the world by the tail. My children were my earthly joy and I had Jesus. I was a stay-at-home mom, and loved having a big family. I believe that one of the highest callings, other than being a child of God, is being a mother.

*Brandy Ann was my first born, a daughter. She had blonde hair, blue eyes and was quiet and mild mannered.

*Taylor was my second born, first son, blonde hair, blue eyes, mischievous and loved to pull pranks on people, then roll with laughter.

*Sara-Frances, third born and the pistol of the bunch. She was always going full speed and wide open, outgoing and never met a stranger. Blue eyes and a smile a mile wide.

*Gus, fourth born, second son. Blonde hair, blue eyes and was in to everything, I refer to him as "that child".

*Mary Alice is the caboose of the bunch. Fifth born, blonde curls and blue eyes. Definitely marches to her own drum.

I love how uniquely different each child was in their personalities. There is nothing more precious to a mother than her children and I am so thankful that God allowed me to be their mama.

One Friday afternoon I picked up my kids from school as usual. We did not live in town so it was about a 25–30-minute drive one way. I remember the conversation on the way home because the next week at school was homecoming which meant they would wear themed outfits each day. We were verbally picking out what Brandy, Taylor and Sara-Frances would be wearing for Western Day on Monday.

Note ~

Gus and Mary Alice were still in car seats,

ages 1 and 2, not old enough for school.

Brandy was 10 and in the 4th grade.

Taylor was 8 and in the 2nd grade

Sara-Frances was 6 and in 1st grade.

The ride home usually consisted of a myriad of topics and conversation. That particular Friday was no different. Except it was, and I was unaware that this would be the last day I would ever pick up my oldest three children from school again.

You see by the time Monday rolled around I was having to pick out three caskets for my beautiful children. On Sunday afternoon in the amount of time it took for a drunk driver to cross the center yellow line of an Alabama highway, my life as I knew it was turned completely upside down.

Brandy, Taylor and Sara-Frances were all killed when the vehicle they were in was struck head on (the drunk driver was killed as well). That day I began a journey that I did not ask for.

This time, this beautiful day in October of 1997, this day that the enemy, the evil one, the ruler of darkness came calling – this day, he had made it all too personal.

Out of all the times the enemy had filtered ugliness and trials throughout my life- many of those I did not know Jesus. This time was different. This time I knew my Jesus and was armed and dangerous (to the darkness of this world). This time, the enemy would not have the victory he thought he would get from such a heinous act on one of God's own.

If the God I serve would allow such a horrific event, I knew it was only because He could and would see me through- with the pain defying power that can only come from Him. I knew I could not do this on my own but by the power of my Christ, and I would give God all the glory.

You see, I am one of the weakest people you will ever meet, but where I am weak my God is strong and lends His strength to me. God gets all the glory! The enemy was barking up the wrong tree when he came calling after me and mine. My children are dancing down streets of gold and I will see them once again because I belong to the King of Kings. My story did not end the day of the wreck, nor the day I buried my children. What the enemy used in hopes of making me ineffective ~ well, instead it ignited a God given gumption and I will proclaim Jesus, Jesus, Jesus until my final breath.

I know firsthand how vital it is to be in God's Word and to walk with Him closely because -Life can stink but my God is good!!! He knew the day I walked down the aisle and asked Jesus to be Lord of my life that

I would one day cling to Him something fierce. I had no clue, but He did.

For everything you and I don't know or could not humanly survive emotionally – our God knows and He can see us through.

This does not mean that you won't walk through the valley of the shadow of death, goodness, I have left foot prints there and at times been knee deep trudging my way through. You may still walk through the fire and you will even feel the heat, but when you have Jesus, when you come out, there is no smell of smoke. There is an unbelievable peace that truly passes any and all human understanding.

My story is not pretty and is much more of a nightmare than I could ever properly describe. Yet, this is not a story to make you sad. No, my story is all about a victory and my God gets ALL the glory!

These next scriptures are a few of my favs- I can't pick just one. I would love for you to look these up and write them out in your journal.

2 Corinthians 12:9-10

Genesis 50:20

Romans8:28

Philippians 4:7

1 Peter 5:10

Romans 8:37

This book is a way for me to share God's Word and who He is with others while praying they grow closer to the Lord in the process or, maybe even find Jesus the way I did all those years ago in a little church in Frisco City, Al.

We face so many things in this life and I want to share the goodness of God and I am praying others will find His saving grace, forgiveness and the freedom that comes from having a personal relationship with Jesus. The closer you walk with Him, the closer you will feel His presence.

A bigger picture of my story is available in a book, <u>From a Mother's Heart- a story of Tragedy and Hope</u>   available on Amazon

My disclaimer: 1 Corinthians 2:2

1 Corinthians 2:2

²For I determined not to know anything among you

except Jesus Christ and Him crucified

Christian Title ~ Christian Life

To be very clear, this is not a study of "feel good fluff". This study is about the grittiness of life and God's grace. It's about a God given gumption that can birth a holy indignation when the enemy targets our families. This study is about the One place you and I can find hope, peace and a sound mind, all because we belong to Jesus Christ. This book is for the Christ followers who want to seek Jesus with intention.

Maybe, for some of you, this study is more about a rededication to Jesus. This would be a great way to begin a rededicated journey with your Jesus. Perhaps you want to know more about this One they call Jesus and what He has to offer. Either way, I invite you to let's Dig in and see where it all leads.

 I will not assume that everyone is a Christ follower who picks up this book. If you are - Hallelujah and let's Dig in – If you have not made this life-altering choice ~ Today is a beautiful day to do so and it would be a decision that you would NEVER regret.

It's as simple as believing the following statements and understanding that you are a mess and need a Savior.

*Jesus is God's Son

*Jesus was born of a virgin

*Jesus died for my sins.

*On the third day, Jesus rose from the dead and is alive today.

*Jesus is coming back.

*Jesus offers forgiveness!

If you believe the above statements, all you need to do is just ask Jesus to be Lord of your life. Either way, I encourage you to Dig in as you may have questions answered along the way.

The truth is that there is nothing more profound yet simple as the Gospel of Jesus Christ.

Life is not easy, and to know there is this One they call Jesus who can help us change our ways ("For all have sinned and fall short of the glory of God" Romans 3:23) because sometimes life will come at us harder than usual. It is in these times that we need to know how to deal with these times and where and to Whom to turn, and the most beautiful part is that we will never be alone during these difficult times.

When we come to know Jesus personally, having asked Him into our heart and become blood bought, born again believers and are following Christ –--the enemy knows. The enemy understands that we are on the winning team, team Victory. The enemy knows this even if we never publicly announced it and were never baptized (please know that even though it is not baptism that saves us and gives eternal life, it is Jesus and only Jesus. I do believe in baptism as it is a beautiful picture not only to others, but for the individual- there is just something about coming up and out of that water, knowing you have been forgiven and you will not spend eternity in hell) Whew, I could spend endless pages going on about that! Just know, the enemy knows!

The enemy becomes well aware, because when we accept Jesus as our Savior, He seals us (marks us as His). I love that the underworld of darkness fully understands Who I belong to!

Ephesians 1:13

¹³In Him you have trusted, after you heard the word of truth,

the gospel of your salvation; in whom also, having believed,

you were sealed with the Holy Spirit …

_____

_____

_____

_____

_____

_____

Ephesians 4:30

³⁰ And do not grieve the Holy Spirit of God,

by whom you were sealed for the day of redemption.

_____
_____
_____
_____

For me, it is an incredibly beautiful picture knowing that when the enemy looks at me, even with all of my faults and wrong choices, and mistakes in life – that the enemy sees me as sealed by Jesus Christ and that I am covered in His righteousness. I like to picture that when the enemy looks at me, he has to put on shades.

You see, when we belong to Jesus Christ, the enemy can NOT have our souls, so his mission is to render us ineffective.

This is why the enemy targets our minds, whispering lies, confusing us and targeting our families. Wearing us down and throwing out tragedy, grief and bad diagnoses and hardship like it's a game of darts.

DO NOT let the enemy win. We have that choice so choose today to allow God to get all the glory.

Joshua 24:15b

15b But as for me and my house,

we will serve the Lord.

_____

_____

_____

Acts 4:12

There is salvation in no one else, for there is no other name

under heaven given to people by which

we must be saved.

_____

_____

_____

True deliverance only comes through Jesus Christ.

As a blood bought believer, you have been set apart and called to a higher standard than those who are of the world. Somewhere along the way many have stopped acting like they are set apart and have fallen victim to going through the motions of checking a box – of reading a devotional, going to church and the buck stops there.

Food for thought ~ If someone were to ask you, "are you a Christian", would you say yes? Many of you would and hopefully you are. Or would you say yes because your family goes to church? Or would you say yes because we live in a "Christian" nation? As a Sunday School teacher that I had many years ago would say – "maybe it's time to do a gut check". I like to think of it as a heart check.

If the above felt familiar, is it time to stop riding the coattails of parents, grandparents or Uncle Joe? Maybe it is time for you to make your own commitment?

If you have accepted Jesus as your Lord and Savior, please know that nothing can take that away from you! Your salvation is secure!

John 10:28

²⁸ And I give them eternal life, and they shall never perish; neither shall anyone snatch them out of My hand.

_____

_____

_____

_____

If you are a Christian but do not spend time cultivating your personal relationship with Him, then you have become a casual Christian/spiritually asleep and you are missing out on so much. Yes, you will spend eternity in heaven but, how fulfilling and beautiful would it be to know we had a part in helping further God's Kingdom. Personally, I want the "so much more" that Jesus gives. That personal relationship that steady's my faith. That gives me confidence in knowing that I know Victory in spite of trials and tribulation.

Victory ~ the act of defeating an enemy or opponent in battle.

1 Corinthians 15:54b-57

54b ... "Death is swallowed up in victory."

55 "O Death, where is your sting?" O Hades, where is your victory?"

56 The sting of death is sin, and the strength of sin is in the law

57 But thanks be to God, who gives us the victory through

our Lord Jesus Chris.

_____

_____

_____

_____

_____

_____

We serve a God of "so much more", a God of exceedingly abundantly above all!

Ephesians 3:20

20 Now to Him who is able to do exceedingly abundantly

above all that we ask or think,

according to the power that works in us,

_____

_____

_____

_____

_____

If you are truly seeking more of Him then I am so excited to have you digging in to God's Word along with me in this study. When you accepted Jesus as your Lord and Savior but found that you really did not know where to go from there and have found yourself just going through the motions, then I am so glad you picked up this book. It's time to get premeditated with your purpose.

Would you ever only claim to have the title of your work job, yet never really show up? As a wife would you claim the title and never be a helper to your husband?

When you got that job – your priorities shifted and you made sure you were in tune with what the job expected of you. When you became a married woman, your husband became a priority (I have no doubt as your fiancé; he was a priority) and of course when that sweet baby was born. Oh, my goodness how your priorities shifted once again.

If you accepted Jesus as a child and it is pretty much all you have ever known, then you may have found it is easy to become complacent. That can be the same if you have been a long-time follower of Christ. Complacency is not our friend.

Have you found yourself caught up in the hustle and bustle of life and your time with the Lord has fallen to the wayside and you are not sure how to get back on track? This study is a great place to start.

This is a beautiful time to have a heart-to-heart conversation with your Lord and share that your passion has waned. Believe me, He already knows but when you have identified and acknowledged this – He can do a mighty work on that heart of yours.

However, when you find Jesus as a young adult it is a little different as you are finding your way and learning to spread your wings. Depending on your lifestyle when you encounter and accept Jesus would depend on how radically things change for you.

If you find that the passion has faded and you are merely going through the motions, and you're finding that everything else (work spouse, children, iPhone, self-gratification, self, etc.) are the things taking priority over your taking time to draw near to God~ This may be a time for you to reflect and "dig in" to His Word. Reminding yourself just Who God is and who you are in Him. Ask Him who He is and be amazed as He shows you.

Pray! Talk with Him, asking Him to remind you of who He is and who you are in Him and to give you a fresh and renewed passion for Him and His Word.

You see, we are not called to be lukewarm – have you ever seen a lukewarm witness or warrior? No, they are passionate and on fire for their cause.

Revelation 3: 15-16

15I know your works, that you are neither cold nor hot.

I could wish you were cold or hot. 16 So then,

because you are lukewarm, and neither cold nor hot,

I will vomit you out of My mouth.

_____

_____

_____

_____

_____

_____

_____

So, have you asked Jesus to be Lord of your life? It is through Him and only Him that you can be saved. It is as simple as asking Him and turning from your old ways to walk in a new and beautiful way with Jesus. Have you realized you are a sinner in need of a Savior? Are you sealed with the Holy Spirit?

Whether you are rededicating your walk with Jesus or you are a brand-new believer, I am excited to be on this journey with you and am praying for a fresh fire to ignite a passion within you for the One we call Jesus.

Let's put some rubber on the road with your walk with this One they call Jesus, My Jesus.

If you have ANY question about becoming a new believer in Jesus Christ, I would love for you to reach out to your Pastor, or myself. If you do not have a Pastor, I highly recommend you find a **Bible** believing church.

My email is southernandunshackled@gmail.com

Let's Dig In

Many people, refer to their time spent reading the Bible or one-on-one time with the Lord as "quiet time". I have never been fond of this term. Maybe it reminds me of the times in my childhood I had to stand in the corner and be quiet. I am not sure. I suppose it could be that I don't use that term because my time with Him and in His Word is not always "quiet", sometimes I end up crying, sometimes I burst into praise. Yes, to sit and be still usually requires some quiet, but for me, there has been out bursts of praise, weeping, singing and so I usually just say that I am "digging in" to God's word or it is my "Sit and Seek" time.

There is not a right or wrong term. What is important is that it is done and repeated often. For this study I will refer to it as, "Digging in" or "sitting and seeking".

To sit usually refers to being still and to seek refers to the attempt of finding something. So, it may seem odd to suggest that someone sit still while seeking something. However, this is exactly what I am talking about. I will note that often to "be still" is a matter of calming your mind/thoughts.

The Bible asks us to do this very thing.

In **Isaiah 46:10** it says to– *Be still and know that I am God.*

In **Matthew 7:7-8** we hear – *seek and ye shall find...*

In other words, it is in the stillness and in the quiet, when we are tuning in and listening that we hear from and experience the Lord Jesus. It is this same Jesus, my Jesus in whom you will also find peace.

When we are intentional about both, seeking Him and being still, it is only then that we experience so much more with our Lord. This is the cultivation part of your relationship with Jesus. This is a beautiful place where you can grow your relationship, knowledge and love for the One who loves you like no other.

Women are usually strategic planners. We meticulously plan so many things only to end up saying that we don't have time for God, His Word, or praying. But goodness, can we plan an outfit for that special occasion, or a themed birthday party for our children. Even the unorganized person uses an awful lot of time and mental space for how to do things.

What if we shifted our mindset and our usual way of doing things and began to be premeditated and planned with intention and purpose.

What if you knew it meant the difference between having peace or not, walking in a confidence that the world does not understand?

Ignite ~ to catch fire, to start burning.

In **Jeremiah 20:9** Jeremiah faced a lot of opposition and he is complaining and saying that he is not even going to mention His (God) name. He's done and just plumb mad at God. However, God's word was in his heart, and trying to contain it only wearied him and Jeremiah found he could hold it back no longer.

Jeremiah 20:9

⁹...But His word was in my heart like a burning fire

shut up in my bones; I was weary of holding

it back and I could not.

_____
_____
_____
_____

Let's spend some time with the Lord and may our love for God's word ignite within us as a burning fire shut up in our bones. Let's get ignited about our Jesus and all He has for us.

And so, with all that being said – where should we start? I am oh so glad you asked. Let's begin with God and the Bible ~ Himself and His very Word.

~~~~~~~~~~~~~~~~~~~~~~~~~~~~~~~~~~

Grab a notebook and pen, and let's have an open and prayerful heart for what God wants to show you.

I have provided a place to write out the scriptures but you may prefer to use a notebook as well.

My hope is that you will begin this study praying about what God would have you to glean from it all. I pray that you will begin each day asking the Holy Spirit for understanding of the scriptures that you will be pouring through.

So, let's sit, seek, dig in and get ignited for the Kingdom; let's seek Jesus with intention!

Week One

~ *God and His Word* ~

In the beginning was the Word, and the Word was with God

and the Word was God   John 1:1

The Bible is far more than just another book. The Bible is a book of history, it's full of fantastic action, violence and peppered with romance. It's a thriller, it's a love story and has stories of coming home, death and resurrections.

This book, the Book of books is life changing and there is none other like it.

Mind blowing right?! The Author and the book are one so, when we pick up our Bible and read, we are interacting with our very God, the Great I Am.

It was man who took quill in hand and wrote the words on parchment. However, those words were inspired by our Holy God.

Let's take a look at some versus of scripture that show us this. I encourage you to write the scripture out by hand on the lines provided or in a notebook. There is something beautiful about writing it down. If you are using a different version of the Bible than the NKJV then you may want to write out the version you are using.

2 Timothy 3: 16-17

16All Scripture is given by inspiration of God, and is profitable

for doctrine, for reproof, for correction, for instruction

in righteousness 17 that the man of God may be complete,

thoroughly equipped for every good work.

_____

_____

_____

_____

_____

NKJV uses the phrase *"Given by inspiration of God"*

NIV uses the term *"God Breathed"*

Both versions get the point across but I love the latter because in Genesis, God breathed life into man. So, for me this is a beautiful picture of Him breathing life into His Word and it coming alive the way man did when He breathed life into him.

Genesis 2:7

7And the Lord God formed man of the dust of the ground,

and breathed into his nostrils the breath of life;

and man became a living being.

_____

_____

_____

_____

The very breath of God causes life to spring forth, WOW!! May God's breath fall fresh on us and our love for Him ignite!!

2 Peter 1: 20-21

20Knowing this first, that no prophecy of Scripture is

of any private interpretation, 21 for prophecy never came

by will of man, but holy men of God spoke

as they were moved by the Holy Spirit.

_____

_____

_____

_____

John 1:14

14And the Word became flesh and dwelt among us,
and we have seen His glory, as the only begotten of the Father,
full of grace and truth.

_____

_____

_____

People will disappoint us and as you are well aware - honesty and truthfulness are often lacking. When people disappoint you, just remember that God never will.

God and the Bible are one and completely inerrant and infallible. The Bible is where we will find pure Truth. His Truth.

John 17:17

17 Sanctify them by Your truth. Your word is truth.

_____

_____

When we know the Truth, we are better equipped at spotting what is not the truth even when it has been presented as truth, which the enemy is good at. We mustn't forget that the enemy often disguises himself. God's Word sheds light on the darkness even when that darkness is disguised as light.

2 Corinthians 11:14

14And no wonder! For satan himself transforms

himself into an angel of light.

_____

_____

_____

Being "still" actually calms us. This is so important for us because sometimes we are pushed and pulled in so many directions we end up creating our own storms.

It's often in the still and quiet places that God reminds us of who He is and it's in the quiet/still places He shows us who we are in Him.

Psalm 107:28-29

28Then they cry out to the Lord in their trouble, and

He brings them out of their distresses. 29 He calms the storm,

so that the waves are still.

_____

_____

_____

_____

Isaiah 30:15

15 For thus says the Lord God, the Holy one of Israel:

"In returning and rest you shall be saved;

In quietness and confidence shall be your strength. ...

_____

_____

_____

The rest of that scripture says, "but you would not". So, we are given a choice.

I feel it is safe to say, many times, in our lives we have not made the right choice; I sure have not. I have reached a point in my life where, whether out of necessity or desperation, I have realized I must be intentional about my decisions, especially when it comes to one-on-one time with my God.

In this attention deficit world, it can be so easy to make knee-jerk decisions and/or just follow the masses. It takes a conscientious intentionality to just stop and take a few steady breaths before moving forward on something. Your whole being reaps the benefits of stilling your mind and body.

I love *Isaiah 30:15*. I don't know about you but I am motivated by the whole rest, quiet, confidence and goodness gracious I will take all the strength I can get!

Let's face it, some days we need more strength than on others.

Being still does not always mean we are resting but often, resting means we are being still. When we rest, our bodies and minds use this time to reset and recover. It's a mending of the mind if you will and time with God is the key.

Take time to write out what you are hoping will come from spending time with God and His Word. If you are not sure, share that with God as well. Write out anything you may be struggling with. Write a prayer asking for Him to help you with this.

_____

_____

_____

_____

_____

_____

_____

_____

_____

_____

_____

_____

_____

_____

_____

~Going Deeper ~

Let's delve deeper into God, my God, the Everlasting God, the Lord, the Creator of the ends of the earth, the Holy One, the Almighty, the Great I Am.

GOD is:

Omnipotent	Infinite
Omnipresent	Jealous
Merciful	Loving
Faithful	Wise
Eternal	Good
Gracious	Holy

He is so much more than what I have listed here, but these are the attributes that we will hone in on for now and we will touch on some others in the coming weeks.

Omnipotent ~ having unlimited power; can do anything.

Matthew 19:26

26 *But Jesus looked at them and said to them*

"With men this is impossible, but with God

all things are possible."

_____

_____

_____

_____

Job 42:1-2

1 *Then Job answered the Lord and said:* 2 *I know*

that You can do everything and that no purpose of Yours

can be withheld from You.

_____

_____

_____

_____

Jeremiah 32:27

27 Behold, I am the Lord, the God of all flesh.

Is there anything too hard for Me.

There is not anything that God can't do. God is all-powerful. There is no limit to His strength. This is Who I want on my side and to have my back!

<u>Omnipresent</u> ~everywhere at the same time.

Proverbs 15:3

3 The eyes of the Lord are in every place, Keeping watch

on the evil and the good.

Psalm 139:7-10

7 Where can I go from Your Spirit? Or where can I flee

from Your presence? 8 If I ascend into heaven,

You are there; If I make my bed in hell,

behold, You are there [9] *If I take the wings of the morning,*

and dwell in the uttermost parts of the sea,

[10] *Even there Your hand shall lead me,*

and your right hand shall hold me.

_____
_____
_____
_____
_____
_____
_____
_____
_____
___
Jeremaiah 23:23-24

[23] *"Am I a God near at hand", says the Lord, "And not a God afar off?*

[24] *Can anyone hide himself in secret places, so I shall not see him?"*

says the Lord; "Do I not fill heaven and earth?"

says the Lord

_____
_____
_____
_____

There is no place that we can go that God is not already there. He is everywhere. His presence fills both heaven and earth, and that is so beautiful to me.

Merciful ~ compassionate, withholding well deserved punishment.

Psalm 145:9

9 The Lord is good to all, and His tender mercies

are over all His works.

_____

_____

_____

Titus 3:5-6

5 Not by works of righteousness which we have done,

but according to His mercy He saved us, through the washing

of regeneration and renewing of the Holy Spirit,

6 whom He poured out on us abundantly

through Jesus Christ our Savior

_____

_____

_____

_____

_____

Psalm 25:10

[10] All the paths of the Lord are mercy and truth,

to such as keep His covenant

and His testimonies.

_____

_____

_____

_____

Lamentations 3:22-23

[22] Through the Lords's mercies we are not consumed,

because His compassions fail not. [23] They are new every morning;

Great is Your faithfulness.

_____

_____

_____

_____

We don't deserve His goodness and yet, He never fails to shower us with His mercy. Every day He is faithful to lavish us with this mercy of His. Have you thanked Him lately for His mercy?

Psalm 136:26

26 Oh, give thanks to the God of heaven!

For His mercy endures forever.

Faithful ~ loyal, steadfast.

2 Timothy 2:13

13 If we are faithless, He remains faithful;

He cannot deny Himself.

Deuteronomy 7:9

9 Therefore know that the Lord your God,

He is God, the faithful God who keeps covenant and mercy

for a thousand generations with those who love Him...

Hebrews 10:23

23 Let us holdfast the confession of our hope without wavering,

for He who promised is faithful.

_____

_____

_____

God is Faithful! He is completely devoted to you, His plan and His purpose. He is not capable of being disloyal.

Eternal ~lasting or existing forever; without beginning or end.

Habakkuk 1:12

12 Are You not from everlasting, O Lord my God...

_____

_____

Revelation 1:8

8 "I am the Alpha and the Omega, the Beginning and the End",

says the Lord, "who is and who was and who is to come,

the Almighty."

_____

_____

_____

_____

God was, God is and He always will be.

<u>_Gracious_</u> ~unmerited favor and forgiveness; undeserved goodness.

Psalm 145:8

[8] *The Lord is gracious and full of compassion,*

Slow to anger and great in mercy.

_____

_____

_____

Isaiah 30:18

[18] *Therefore the Lord will wait, that He may be gracious to you;*

and therefore He will be exalted, that He may have mercy

on you. For the Lord is a God of justice;

Blessed are all those who wait for Him.

_____

_____

Ephesians 2:8

8For by grace you have been saved through faith,

and that not of yourselves; it is the gift of God

James 4:6

6But He gives more grace. Therefore He says:

"God resists the proud, but gives grace to the humble."

John 1:16-17

16And of His fullness we have all received grace for grace.

17For the law was given through Moses,

but grace and truth came through Jesus Christ.

I am so thankful for His grace that I do not deserve.

Infinite~ limitless, endless in space. Impossible to measure.

Romans 11:33-36

33 *Oh, the depth of the riches both of the wisdom*

and knowledge of God!

How unsearchable are His judgments

and His ways past finding out!

34 *For who has known the mind of the Lord?*

Or who has become His counselor?

35 *Or who has first given to Him and it shall*

be repaid to him? 36 *For of Him and through Him*

and to Him are all things, to whom be glory forever.

Amen.

_____

_____

_____

_____

_____

_____

_____

Isaiah 40:28

²⁸ Have you not known? Have you not heard?

The everlasting God, the Lord, The Creator of the ends of the earth,

neither faints nor is weary. His understanding is unsearchable.

_____

_____

_____

_____

Psalm 147:5

⁵ Great is our Lord, and mighty in power;

His understanding is infinite.

_____

_____

_____

God has NO Limits, we do and the enemy does but our God does not!

<u>Jealous</u> ~ fiercely protective of one's possessions.

Exodus 20:5

⁵ you shall not bow down to them nor serve them.

For I the Lord your God, am a jealous God...

_____

_____

_____

Deuteronomy 4:24

24 For the Lord your God is a consuming fire,

a jealous God.

_____

_____

_____

Psalm 79:5

5How long Lord? Will You be angry forever?

Will Your jealousy burn like fire?

_____

_____

_____

Psalm 78:58

58 For they provoked Him to anger with their high places,

and moved Him to jealousy with their carved images.

_____

_____

_____

We serve a jealous God. We are His. We are to worship no other gods. He is the One True God and He deserves ALLLL the praise and glory.

Loving ~ expresses strong, deep affection and care.

John 3:16

[16] *For God so loved the world that He gave His only begotten Son, that whoever believes in Him should not perish but have everlasting life.*

_____
_____
_____
_____

1 John 4:16

[16] *And we have known and believed the love that God has for us. God is love and he who abides in love abides in God, and God in him.*

_____
_____
_____
_____

Ephesians 2:4-5

4 But God, who is rich in mercy, because of His great Love

with which He loved us 5 even when we were dead in trespasses,

made us alive together with Christ

_____

_____

_____

_____

His love is amazing. His love never fails and His love is endless.

Wise ~ knowledge and good judgement.

Isaiah 55:8-9

8 "For My thoughts are not your thoughts,

Nor are your ways My ways," says the Lord.

9 "For as the heavens are higher than the earth,

so are My ways higher that your ways

and My thoughts than your thoughts.

_____

_____

_____

_____

_____

Proverbs 3:19-20

[19] The Lord by wisdom founded the earth;

by understanding He established the heavens;

[20] By His knowledge the depths were broken up,

and clouds drop down the dew.

_____

_____

_____

_____

We can rest in the assurance that God is wise and is strategic in all the ways He uses His knowledge.

Good ~ morally right, righteous.

Psalm 34:8

[8] Oh taste and see that the Lord is good;

Blessed is the man who trusts in Him!

_____

_____

_____

Psalm 107:1

¹ Oh, give thanks to the Lord, for He is good!

For His mercy endures forever!

_____

_____

_____

Through the trials and tragedies that I have seen in my life, I have come to the realization that ~ Life can stink but God is still good!

Holy ~ consecrated, spiritually perfect and pure.

Leviticus 19:2

² "Speak to all the congregation of the children of Israel,

and say to them: You shall be holy,

for I the Lord your God am holy.

_____

_____

_____

_____

Revelation 4:8

[8] The four living creatures, each having six wings,

were full of eyes around and within.

And they do not rest day or night, saying;

"Holy, holy, holy,

Lord God Almighty,

Who was and is and is to come!"

_____

_____

_____

_____

_____

1 Peter 1:15-16

[15] but as He who called you is holy,

you also be holy in all your conduct,

[16] because it is written,

"Be holy, for I am holy.

_____

_____

_____

_____

1 Samuel 2:2

2 No one is holy like the Lord, For there is none besides You,

Nor is there any rock like our God.

_____

_____

_____

Pure and simple, God is holy. I don't know about you but I am in utter awe of my God. I praise God that He is exactly Who He says He is.

Was there anything about Who God is that was new to you? How would you describe Him? How does your view of God today differ from when you were a small child? If you still are not sure, write out a prayer asking God to show you exactly Who He is.

_____

_____

_____

_____

_____

_____

_____

_____

_____

_____

_____

_____

_____

_____

_____

_____

Week Two

~ Your Worth ~

Consider how precious a soul must be when

both God and the devil are after it

Charles Spurgeon

The Lord God formed you and knew you before you were ever in your mother's womb. Oh, how precious you and the details of your life are to Him. He is innately aware of every single thing that breaks your heart.

God doesn't create mediocre. He created you with such detail and purpose. He created you in His image. When we understand who we are in Christ, we have a greater understanding of our worth to the Kingdom. Not the worth that the world places on us but the worth that our Lord Jesus has placed on and within us.

He made you soft and beautiful. He created you to be caring and nurturing, yet He gave you a firm stance when needed. A strong and mighty inner "mama bear mode" as some call it. I don't believe you have to be a mother to have this. I believe it is a part of what makes up a woman just as God has given you acute intuition, which is often a great help to our husbands.

I believe that this mama bear mode is actually a God given gumption that will rise to the occasion, and be unleashed if say, someone were to come after your children.

When the enemy is in attack mode and our husbands, children, or grandchildren are the target – this is where that God given gumption gives birth to a holy indignation. So, we better make sure we are in tune with God and that we are not reacting from our flesh.

The Lord gave you a strong and sound mind. You are a marvelous work of His creation. You have been forgiven, redeemed, restored, equipped and highly favored and so much more. Let's take a look at what God says about you, His beloved.

I would suggest you begin each of these with "I am"

Forgiven

Redeemed

Restored

Called

Equipped

Highly favored

Created in His Image

Fearfully made

Wonderfully made

More than a conqueror

Master piece

Strong

Chosen

Justified

Sealed

Psalm 139:13-14

[13] *For You formed my inward parts; You covered*

me in my mother's womb. [14] *I will praise You*

for I am fearfully and wonderfully made.

_____

_____

_____

_____

Psalm 103:12

[12] *As far as the east is from the west,*

So far has He removed our transgressions from us.

_____

_____

_____

Ephesians 1:7

[7] *In Him we have redemption through His blood,*

the forgiveness of sins, according to

the riches of His grace.

_____

_____

_____

_____

Isaiah 43:1-3

[1]...Fear not, for I have redeemed you;

I have called you by your name;

You are Mine.

[2] When you pass through the waters, I

Will be with you;

And through the rivers, they shall not

Overflow you.

When you walk through the fire, you

Shall not be burned,

Nor shall the flame scorch you.

[3] For I am the Lord your God...

_____

_____

_____

_____

_____

_____

_____

_____

_____

_____

_____

1 Peter 5:10

10 But the God of all grace, who called us to His eternal glory

by Christ Jesus, after you have suffered a while,

perfect, establish, strengthen, and settle you.

_____
_____
_____
_____

This scripture, 1 Peter 5;10 is one of my favorites. Having walked through the fire myself, it hits home and I am both thankful for His promises and cling to them something fierce!

You are called and you are chosen ~ do not take this lightly.

Romans 1:6

6Among whom you also are the called of Jesus Christ

_____
_____

1 Peter 2:9

9 But you are a chosen generation, a royal priesthood,

a holy nation. His own special people, that you may proclaim the praises of Him who called you out of darkness

into His marvelous light...

_____

_____

_____

_____

_____

Have you ever felt inferior or just not like everyone else? Maybe you don't struggle with feeling shame or guilt? Maybe you carry a heaviness from many years prior? Call on the above scripture and just remind yourself that you are chosen and have been brought out of the darkness and into His marvelous light.

Hebrews 13:21 (NASB)

[21] Equip you in every good thing to do His will,

working in us that which is pleasing in His sight

through Jesus Christ, to whom

be the glory forever and ever.

Amen

_____

_____

_____

_____

_____

_____

Our Lord equips us as needed. You may be familiar with the saying ~ "God doesn't call the equipped, He equips the called." We need to have full faith and trust in God when we are not sure of ourselves. This means we can be equipped when battles come our way as well, and He wants us leaning in to Him for the equipping as needed. He equips our minds and hearts.

2 Timothy 3:17

[17]That the man of God may be complete,

thoroughly equipped for every good work.

_____

_____

_____

Romans 8:1

[1] There is therefore now no condemnation to those

who are in Christ Jesus, who do not walk according

to the flesh, but according to the Spirit.

_____

_____

_____

_____

This is a reminder of who we are in Christ which means we are living in VICTORY and should not forget that, even though the enemy would sure like us to.

Romans 5:1-2

¹Therefore, having been justified by faith, we have peace

with God through our Lord Jesus Christ,

² Through whom also we have access

by faith into this grace in which we stand,

and rejoice in hope of the glory of God.

_____

_____

_____

_____

_____

1 Corinthians 2:22

²²Who also has sealed us and given us the Spirit

in our hearts as a guarantee.

_____

_____

_____

You my dear one, *are known, forgiven redeemed, chosen, called, justified, thoroughly equipped and sealed*!!!! Hallelujah!!

When you find yourself thinking things about yourself that are not what God says, take time to speak the things that God says about you in His Word. Replacing the lies with the truth.

You were created in His image and remember, God doesn't create mediocre.

Genesis 1:27

27 So God created man in His own image; in the image of God

He created him; male and female

He Created them.

_____

_____

_____

You are valuable, of great worth as the definition reads. You are priceless to your heavenly Father.

Matthew 6:26

[26] Look at the birds of the air, for they neither sow nor reap

nor gather into barns; yet your heavenly Fater feeds them.

Are you not of more value than they?

_____

_____

_____

_____

Jesus calls you friend.

John 15:14-15

[14] You are My friends if you do whatever I command you.

[15] No longer do I call you servants, for a servant does not

know what his master is doing; but I have called you friends,

for all that I have heard from My Father I have made known to you.

_____

_____

_____

_____

_____

_____

You are special to your heavenly Father, remind yourself often.

How do you view yourself? How do you feel about what the God of the universe says and feels about you? Write out a prayer asking God to show you who you are to Him.

_____

_____

_____

_____

_____

_____

_____

_____

_____

_____

_____

_____

_____

_____

_____

_____

_____

_____

~ *Finding Rest/Peace*~

Have you ever found yourself going to great lengths to avoid rest, like it is a bad thing? Do you find that after a night of sleep that you still do not feel rested. Or find yourself not stopping and sitting down during the day, almost afraid someone will see you and think you have been doing nothing?

As women, often times we feel guilty about resting but we need rest. We live in a hurry up and let's get busier society, so how in the world are we to find rest? Many times, we are looking in all the wrong places.

For all you brand new mama's out there, or mamas with little ones, yes, I understand! Things, lots of things, become more difficult when you have little ones to take care of.

I could not wait to have a baby and was beyond elated when we discovered I was expecting our first child, only to discover that sleep deprivation was part of the birthing package. Other women had mentioned to me in my later months of pregnancy to be sure and sleep now because sleepless nights were coming for me.

I would just smile when they said this, but honestly, not having experienced real lack of sleep, I could not conceive what they were talking about. I had no clue, until I did.

Sleep deprivation is REAL and it still amazes me to this day how one tiny, little, precious and to this mama, perfect being could cause so much insomnia. Naps, ha! My first born was not keen on a nap either. I never understood why so many would tell me to nap when she napped. Someone needed to explain to her that she was supposed to sleep. She did sleep beautifully as long as she was being driven around, which did nothing for me and my sleep situation.

I did not know my Jesus when I had my first child. So, I felt as though I was out on this limb all by myself. With Jesus, we are never alone, even when things are tough.

Praise God my second child slept through the night and loved to take 3–4-hour naps during the day while his big sister, well, big sister still wasn't sleeping.

I get it, I really do. If you have a house full of littles you are in a different season than the empty nester or someone who has never had children. The Lord is in this season with you and will not leave you.

There is both a resting of the body and then there is a resting of the mind, both are important.

It doesn't help that we have been made to feel as though multi-tasking is worthy of accolades. When we fall for this, there is a price – overwhelm and meltdown of the senses. A weariness of body and spirit and that's just for starters which can lead to a sense of unworthiness and the enemy can use this as an opportunity.

God did not make any mistakes in how He created us. We were created to need the rest and He is the One who can provide true rest. Rest is a requirement and is crucial to our being alert to the enemy.

God Himself set the precedent for rest. He understood the need and what a gift He has given us to be able to rest both body and mind from weariness, hard work or the battles of spiritual warfare.

Genesis 2:2

² And on the seventh day God ended His work

which He had done, and He rested...

_____

_____

_____

Hebrews 4:9-11

⁹There remains therefore a rest for the people of God

.¹⁰ For he who has entered His rest has also ceased from his works

as God did from His. ¹¹Let us therefore be diligent

to enter that rest, lest anyone fall according to the same

example of disobedience.

_____

_____

_____

_____

_____

Matthew 11:28

²⁸Come to Me, all you who labor and are heavy laden,

and I will give you rest.

_____

_____

_____

Psalm 37:7a

⁷ᵃRest in the Lord, and wait patiently for Him

_____

_____

It makes sense that Rest and Peace seem to go hand in hand. Especially when we know that it is in Him that we can find true rest and He is also the One who can give us peace. The peace that passes human understanding. The peace that does not make sense in a world of chaos, pain, suffering and grief.

Romans 12:2

²And do not be conformed to this world, but be transformed

by the renewing of your mind, that you may prove

what is that good and acceptable

and perfect will of God.

_____

_____

_____

_____

_____

I love that this verse in Romans is reminding us to stop thinking as the world does. It is reminding us that we need to be conscious of our thoughts and actions in order for us to realize that we need to, stop and redirect our thoughts toward Him, our Lord. The more focused on the Lord, the fewer knee-jerk reactions and the beautiful side effect is that we will be more in tune with His will.

Intentionally seek Him and His peace!

Psalm 34:14

¹⁴Depart from evil and do good;

Seek peace and purse it

_____

_____

_____

Ephesians 2:14a

14 For He Himself is our peace...

_____

_____

_____

Psalm 29:11

11 The Lord will give strength to His people;

The Lord will bless His people with peace.

_____

_____

_____

2 Peter 1:2-4a

2 Grace and peace be multiplied to you in the knowledge of God

and of Jesus our Lord,3 as His divine power has given

to us all things that pertain to life and godliness,

through the knowledge of Him who called us by glory

and virtue, 4a by which have been given to us exceedingly great and precious promises...

_____

_____

_____

_____

_____

_____

John 14:27

27 Peace I leave with you, My peace I give to you;

not as the world gives do I give to you.

Let not your heart be troubled,

neither let it be afraid.

_____

_____

_____

_____

It is in this time with Him, the leaning in to Him and His rest ~ soaking up this peace that He and only He gives, that allows our weary souls to take a deep breath and reset. This peace is a gift that He wants to bless us with and will even multiply as we intentionally seek Him. It is with this peace that we can begin to understand that we need not fear.

2 Timothy 1:7

7 For God has not given us a spirit of fear,

but of power and of love

and a sound mind.

_____

_____

_____

_____

In this crazy and chaos filled world ~ you my sweet friend were not given a spirit of fear and on top of that you were given: power, love and a sound mind! That makes me want to shout, AMEN!

Some days that scripture hits a little deeper and sweeter. So many of the scriptures do, but unless we spend time in them, meditating on them, we won't know this first hand.

This leaves us with such incredible hope.

Hebrews 6:19

19 This hope we have as an anchor of the soul,

both sure and steadfast...

_____

_____

_____

_____

Jesus knew we would need an anchor, He knew we needed Him. Jesus also knew that we would experience trials while on earth. I love that His Word points us to the knowledge that we can lean in to Him for the peace and rest we so crave, and this is where we realize, He is our anchor. Jesus is the ONLY thing/one that can steady us during tumultuous times.

Take time this week, purposeful time to lean in to your Lord for rest.

How do you feel getting this "rest" and finding peace would shape you differently for those around you? Write out your prayer for what you need in these areas of your life.

_____

_____

_____

_____

_____

_____

_____

_____

_____

_____

_____

_____

_____

Week Three

~ Confidence/Boldness ~

Confidence ~ *feeling or belief that one can rely on someone or something. A firm trust.*

Boldness ~ *Brave, confident, courageous, fearless. A willingness to take risks and act innovatively.*

Has the world or maybe even a relationship, left you feeling hopeless or with a self-worth that would not even register on a meter? Maybe you grew up in a household were you never even received encouragement and instead where belittled? No one ever built you up, encouraged you and you find that you may even be uncomfortable with a compliment because edification is not familiar?

We need to remove all the titles and unworthiness that others and the world have placed on us and we need to focus on who and what the Lord says about us.

We need the confidence that Christ gives us as we deal with life and the things that come our way. Tribulations, trials, adversity, suffering, downright hard moments, agony, grief, distress, pain – the woes of life.

Jesus tells us that we will have these things and not if but when. Our boldness should come from our Lord and knowing that victory has been sealed. When we truly walk in who we are in Christ Jesus ~ we walk differently. We walk in such a way that the world knows we are different. Not cocky but confident and with a God given boldness that comes only from Him.

John 16:33

33 These things I have spoken to you, that in Me

you may have peace.

In the world you will have tribulation;

but be of good cheer,

I have overcome the world.

_____
_____
_____
_____
_____
_____
_____

Acts 4:13

¹³ Now when they saw the boldness of Peter and John,

and perceived that they were uneducated

and untrained men, they marveled.

And they realized that they had been with Jesus.

_____

_____

_____

_____

_____

Can people look at you and understand that you walk with Jesus or that there is something different about you?

Proverbs 28:1

¹The wicked flee when no one pursues,

But the righteous are bold as a lion.

_____

_____

_____

_____

Paul reminds us in Ephesians that we have this boldness and access through confidence through our faith in Jesus.

Ephesians 3:12

¹²in whom we have boldness and access

with confidence through faith in Him

_____

_____

_____

_____

I am shy by nature and I can promise you that I don't have a bold bone in my body. Any and all boldness I have, it comes from the Lord. It has been through precious time spent with Him, that He has given me the boldness I need, and when I need it. Yes, there are times it would be oh so easy to revert back into my shy and pathetic shell where most of my childhood and teen years were spent. However, because I know the truth, that thought is only fleeting and I lean in to my Jesus and the whole **Phillipians 4:13** – *I can do all things through Christ who strengthens me.*

Seek Him and ask Him for boldness, this is what Paul did.

Acts 4:29, 31

29 Now Lord, look on threats, and grant to Your servants

that with all boldness they may speak Your word...

31 And when they had prayed, the place where they

were assembled together was shaken;

and they were all filled with the Holy Spirit,

and they spoke the word of God with boldness.

_____

_____

_____

_____

_____

_____

_____

_____

_____

Something else that takes a boldness ~ obeying God rather than man.

I am a people pleaser and for me being bold, well it is only doable by being in close relationship with my Jesus. We are witnesses for Him, and as His servants, obedience should be a side effect from our love for Him.

Acts 5:29-32

[29] *But Peter and the other apostles answered and said:*

"We ought to obey God rather than men.

[30] *The God of our fathers raised up Jesus*

whom you murdered by hanging on a tree, [31] *Him God has*

exalted to His right hand to be Prince and Savior,

to give repentance to Israel and forgiveness of sins.

[32] *And we are His witnesses to these things, and so also is*

the Holy Spirit whom God has given to those who obey Him."

_____

_____

_____

_____

_____

_____

_____

Let's take a look at a few scriptures in Romans. We will be looking at other scriptures as well but I want to focus on several from here. When I read Romans, especially chapter 8, I am filled with so much confidence!

Confidence is a beautiful thing when it comes from who we are in Christ and not from the worth that the world places on us. Through

Christ, we have the ability to conqueror things that were meant to destroy us. Things intending to wear us down and out, rendering us ineffective.

Romans 5: 3-5

3 And not only that, but we also glory in tribulations, knowing that tribulation produces perseverance; 4 and perseverance, character; and character, hope.5 Now hope does not disappoint, because the love of God has been poured out in our hearts by the Holy Spirit who was given to us.

_____
_____
_____
_____
_____
_____

James 1:3

2My brethren, count it all joy when you fall into various trials,3 knowing that the testing of your faith produces patience.

_____
_____
_____
_____

Life will come and sometimes it will come at you full force! These scriptures in James and Romans let us know that we need to "keep on keepin' on". It doesn't mean that we have to like what is happening one bit. We just need to know that Almighty God will see us through.

There is not ANYTHING that you will face on this earth that the Lord cannot see you through and I know this first hand. We do have the choice of whether or not to let Him. We have to choose to trust, believe, and obey. (we will cover obedience in the last week)

It is a daily choice to trust. Choose wisely.

John 10:10

[10] The thief does not come except to steal,

and to kill, and to destroy.

I have come that they may have life

and that they may have it more abundantly.

_____

_____

_____

_____

_____

The first part of that scripture that says the enemy came to steal, kill and destroy ~ well, that means that he came to rock your world and throw at you something that is humanly impossible to bear! If you have experienced grief or tragedy then you know this for a fact as I do. **BUT**, the second part of this scripture where Jesus Himself tells us that He came to give life and life more abundantly~ well, that means that what the evil one used to rock your world- Jesus can see you through it and give you a peace that passes all understanding. Jesus offers us a pain defying peace, a supernatural peace.

Oh, the confidence we can have because we have our Jesus!

Genesis 50:20

20But as for you, you meant evil against me,

but God meant it for good.

_____

_____

_____

Romans 8:28

28And we know that all things work together for good

to those who love God, to those who are the called

according to His purpose.

_____

_____

_____

_____

In both, *Genesis 50:20* and *Romans 8:28* we see that even when evil is thrown our way, and we belong to Him, God can and will use it for good. I call this, beauty from ashes. God gets all the glory, and so, why would we not want to walk in the knowledge and confidence that our God has our backs?

Romans 8:31

31 What then shall we say to these things?

If God is for us, who can be against us?

_____

_____

_____

Are you feeling the confidence welling up yet?

Romans 8: 37

37 Yet in all these things we are more than conquerors

through Him who loved us.

_____

_____

_____

More than conquerors, WoW! Talk about a confidence builder. This is a scripture I highly recommend that you memorize and repeat often as a beautiful reminder that we have not been left defenseless or powerless.

There will never be a time or experience for us that the Lord will not be with us. It depends on us leaning in to Him during these times for us to feel His incredible presence but He is there for us and eager and ready to guide us. Knowing this, it bolsters my confidence when I face situations that I had rather not be facing. This next scripture is a beautiful example of this.

Isaiah 58:11

¹¹The Lord will guide you continually,

and satisfy your soul in drought, and strengthen your bones;

you shall be like a watered garden, and like a spring of water,

whose waters do not fail.

_____

_____

_____

_____

_____

One of the most powerful things we have, and I believe we take it most for granted, is that the same power that raised Jesus from the grave ~ this power lives in every blood bought, born again, believing Christ follower. We should walk like the daughter of the King that we are. Again, not cocky but with sheer confidence that Jesus Christ, supernaturally can see me through what is humanly impossible to deal with.

Remember, we are set apart and when we belong to Jesus, people will pick up on the fact that we are different. They may not be able to put a finger on why you are different but they know that you and I are.

Yes, we live in a sin filled world and horrible things do take place. But you my dear, you can walk in the bold knowledge that through the power of Jesus Christ ~ you have a supernatural position on this battlefield in this age of warfare.

Galatians 2:20

I have been crucified with Christ; it is no longer I who live,

but Christ lives in me; and the life which I now live in the flesh

I live by faith in the Son of God, who loved me

and gave Himself for me.

_____

_____

_____

_____

After spending time in these scriptures this week, are you feeling more confident? I sure hope so. Be sure and spend time praying and asking the Lord to help restore anywhere that the world has broken your confidence. Ask for boldness. Write out your prayer with confidence knowing that He is listening.

_____
_____
_____
_____
_____
_____
_____
_____
_____
_____
_____
_____
_____
_____
_____
_____
_____
_____
_____

Week Four

~ The enemy/ Armed ~

7And war broke out in heaven: Michael and his angels fought with the dragon; and the dragon and his angels fought 8but they did not prevail, nor was a place found for them in heaven any longer 9 So the great dragon was cast out, that serpent of old, called the devil and satan, who deceives the whole world; he was cast to earth, and his angels were cast out with him.

Revelation 12:7-9

The dragon, master manipulator, the evil one, the enemy, lucifer, satan, the devil; whatever name you use to refer to him, know this – he is real and he is our number one enemy. Our adversary is on a mission and fully understands his self-imposed assignment.

One of the enemy's most frequented targets is our mind; a close second would be our husbands, children and grandchildren. We need a holy indignation when it comes to protecting our families and we need to be battle ready.

We have Jesus so we have no need to fear this enemy. We should however, not underestimate his wickedness and we should be very, very aware of his antics.

1 Peter 5:8

⁸Be sober, be vigilant because your adversary

the devil walks about like a roaring lion,

seeking whom he may devour.

_____

_____

_____

_____

The master manipulator is doing what he does and is on the prowl, always looking for an opportunity. We must be alert.

Being alert means having a clear head and using discernment. Ever been so confused you felt as though you could not think straight? There is a reason for that. Which brings me to our next scripture.

1 Corinthians 14:33

33 For God is not the author of confusion.

But of peace...

_____

_____

_____

Life is going to "life" and at the end of the day, it is so much harder to deal with and "do life" without God. Our Lord is fully aware and tells us over and over, come to Him, and to submit to Him.

Let me be clear, when I say "without" I am not talking about those who do not know Him but those who **do know** who He is and do not have a relationship with Him. Even the devil and demons know and believe there is one God. Believing is one thing ~ asking Jesus into your heart and life is another, this is what gives us full access to God. It is all about your personal relationship with Jesus. A heart knowledge with your Savior and not just a head knowledge of who He is.

James 2:19

19 You believe that there is one God. You do well.

Even the demons believe - and tremble!

_____

_____

_____

The only way to God is through Jesus Christ, His Son. So, knowing that there is a God is very different than having a personal relationship.

John 14:6

Jesus said to him, "I am the way, the truth, and the life.

No one comes to the Father except through Me.

_____

_____

_____

James 4:7-8

7Therefore submit to God. Resist the devil

and he will flee from you.8 Draw near to God

and He will draw near to you...

_____

_____

_____

_____

Remember, the enemy loves to target our mind. Once in the mind the derailing can begin. I believe the second of his targets is our families (husbands, children and grandchildren).

When our holy indignation is fueled, we should be battle ready as to not react in the flesh, but in the Spirit. We also need to understand that through Christ, we have authority over the evil one.

Matthew 28:18

[18] ...All authority has been given to Me

in heaven and on earth.

Titus 2:15

[15]Speak these things, exhort, and rebuke

with all authority...

---

1 Peter 5:9a

[9a]Resist him, steadfast in the faith...

Resisting the devil can be done. We have the power to do just that, resist the devil. Not of our might but through Christ.

There is also power in the name of Jesus. That's right, we need only to call on His name and the underworld is reminded Who we belong to. Call out the name of Jesus and repeat often.

Personally, I call on the name of Jesus in my car, while walking throughout my home and often when on a walk.

Philippians 2:9-11

9 Therefore God also has highly exalted Him

and given Him the name which is above every name,

10 that at the name of Jesus every knee should bow,

of those in heaven, and of those on earth,

and of those under the earth, 11 and that every tongue

should confess that Jesus Christ is Lord,

to the glory of God the Father.

_____

_____

_____

_____

_____

_____

The victory already belongs to Jesus. This doesn't mean that the enemy won't try to give us all "he's got"; he will surely try. Just remember, to Whom you belong – Christ lives in you.

1 John 4:4

⁴He who is in you is greater than he who is in the world.

_____

_____

We must be ready to replace the lies of the enemy with Truth. The enemy loves to whisper lies and he hopes they sink deep into our psyche. Being in God's Word regularly is the only way to be able to combat those lies. Otherwise, we find ourselves befuddled and wanting to return to our unhealthy, abusive and familiar situations and ways of life. Or find we even return to a spiritual slumber and complacency.

Jeremiah 29:12-14a

¹² Then you will call upon Me and go and pray to Me,

and I will listen to you. ¹³ And you will seek Me

and find Me, when you search for Me

with all your heart, ¹⁴ᵃ I will be found by you,

says the Lord...

_____

_____

_____

_____

_____

_____

_____

I know most Christians are familiar with the scripture right before this, _Jeremaiah, 29:11 (_For I know the plans I have for you...) but so often the verses 12-14 are skipped over.

We must diligently seek the Lord in our day to day lives and with ALL of our heart – remember, it is not about checking a box. This is serious business.

THIS IS WARFARE, Spiritual warfare. This is an unseen battle between darkness and Light and I guarantee you that just because you can't "see" it doesn't mean it isn't real.

~ Armed ~

So, we can walk in confidence and we have the power to rebuke, but what about a weapon? The enemy is relentless and we should be as well.

Let's face it, things can get gritty and we need a weapon, right?! Yes, we do and yes, He does! God doesn't leave us hanging, He provides that too.

I used the term "gritty" but it's **Spiritual Warfare** and we enter the battlefield every single day.

God has given His children a strength that the world can't tap into, but you and I can. The most important thing I have found in preparation is to saturate yourself with the Word of God!! When we pour over the scriptures and let them seep in deep, this allows the Lord to pour back into us. This is part of our equipping and this allows us to walk in the confidence and boldness of the Lord.

Let's look at some scriptures that will walk you through key points of arming yourself.

Ephesians 6: 10-13

[10] Finally, my brethren, be strong in the Lord and in the power

of His might. [11] Put on the whole armor of God,

that you may be able to stand against the wiles of the devil.

[12] For we do not wrestle against flesh and blood,

but against principalities, against powers,

against the rulers of the darkness of this age,

against spiritual hosts of wickedness in the heavenly places.

[13] Therefore take up the whole armor of God,

that you may be able to withstand in the evil day,

and having done all, to stand.

_____

_____

_____

_____

_____

_____

_____

_____

_____

_____

Here in Ephesians, we are told that it is the Lord's strength and His might that we use to fight the battles that we will be faced with, and not of our own strength. But to do so we need to understand exactly what it is we are fighting against.

The master manipulator, the enemy, the devil, the ruler of darkness of this age. He is pure prime evil and he is very crafty and good at what he does. That is all fine and dandy because we have Jesus and the whole armor of God that can stand against the wiles of our enemy, the devil and we have the assurance that if we use this armor, that we will be able to withstand.

That makes me want to break into a chorus of "Standing on the promises of God". I can't sing so I won't but, in my head, I am going to town on that song.

*In **Ephesians**, verses 14-18 we are told to:*

[14]Gird your waist with truth

Put on the breastplate of righteousness

[15]Shod your feet with the gospel of peace

***16** —ABOVE ALL, taking up the shield of faith with which you will be able to quench ALL the fiery darts of the wicked one*

[17]And take the helmet of salvation, and the

Sword of the Spirit which is the word of God.

[18]Pray always.

Each of these are vital but take an extra hard look at verse 16. It says "ABOVE ALL" and then goes on to say that this shield will quench "ALL" the fiery darts of the wicked one.

1 John 4:4

4 You are of God, little children, and have overcome them,

because He who is in you is greater than he who is in the world.

_____

_____

_____

_____

Mic drop!! Take that devil.

Are you still asking why should we be armed? It's what warriors do and God does not leave us defenseless. He gives us both armor and a weapon.

However, a weapon is only useful if we use it. We have choice.

So, how does one use this weapon...

First, it must be picked up!

If your Bible sits on a shelf, nightstand, or coffee table and is never picked up it won't be as effective.

If it is only picked up when you leave for church, it won't be as effective.

If you are reading a sweet little devotional instead of God's word, it won't be as effective.

Please know I am not against a good devotional; I love a good one. A devotional should be used as a compliment to God's word, not in place of.

Hebrews 4:12

[12] For the word of God is living and powerful,

and sharper than any two-edged sword,

piercing even to the division of soul and spirit...

_____

_____

_____

_____

Goodness, I love this verse! The word of God is living and powerful (the NASB version uses the word active instead of powerful) either word paints a powerful picture.

The antics of the enemy need a light so we can see it for what it is ~ a wile of the devil himself.

Christ is our light and the Holy Spirit gives us discernment.

John 8:12

[12] Then Jesus spoke to them again saying,

"I am the light of the world. He who follows Me

shall not walk in darkness, but have the light of life."

_____

_____

_____

_____

John 1:4-5

[4] In Him was life and the life was the light of men.

[5] And the light shines in the darkness,

and the darkness did not comprehend it.

_____

_____

_____

_____

_____

Jesus is our light that we call on to cast out the darkness. Remember, the very name of Jesus is powerful and nothing replaces being in His Word and saturating ourselves with His very Word. Reading it out loud. Writing it and yes, even memorization is important.

When we belong to Jesus and are sealed with the Holy Spirit and we have an authority over the enemy.

Hebrews 4:16

16 Let us therefore come boldly to the throne of grace,

that we may obtain mercy and find grace to help in time of need.

(the NASB says "let us draw near with confidence")

_____

_____

_____

We serve a Savior who has given us FULL access and that we may be bold and confident in who we are in Him. The enemy shudders when we exercise this access we have with our Jesus! The evil one wants us to be small in our faith, fearful and timid, hiding in a corner like a small child.

The cross, this is when and where we were able to gain this full access. Prior to the cross there were sacrifices, a high priest and there was a veil that separated us from God.

Fast forward a few hundred years and a whole lot of silence from God~ then a precious cry from a mere babe breaks more than the silence and begins an immanent trek towards the tearing of the veil. Enter JESUS! Oh, what beautiful praises! On the cross, Jesus became the ultimate sacrifice for you and I.

While Jesus was on the cross, a darkness fell over all the land. The ground shook, rocks split and the veil tore in two. It tore from the top to the bottom and not a thread held it anywhere. We had just gained full access.

Matthew 27:45, 51

45 Now from the sixth hour until the ninth hour there was a darkness over all the land...51 Then, behold, the veil of the temple was torn in two from top to bottom and the earth quaked, and the rocks were split...

_____

_____

_____

_____

_____

We have FULL ACCESS and the devil is aware of this and is not happy about it; he attempts to make us feel as though we can't come boldly to the throne of grace! The more we are in God's Word for ourselves, the less likely we will be to fall for another one of the enemy's tricks.

It is our responsibility, and we each have the choice whether to get serious. After all, this is serious business. As someone who claims the title of being a Christian, we once again can just give lip service or we can walk in confidence and be the witnesses and warriors we were called to be for our families and the Kingdom of Christ. This is why we have a weapon; weapons are what warriors use.

We need the confidence that Christ gives us as we deal with life and the things that come our way. Tribulations, trials, adversity, suffering, downright hard moments, agony, grief, distress, pain – the woes of life if you will. Jesus tells us that we will have these things, and not if but when.

I love to write out scripture and I also love to read it aloud. One thing that most people do not enjoy is memorization of scripture. Folks, memorizing scripture is not something you will regret. I heard someone say once that when we are able to recall scripture, it unleashes the power of God. I believe this because I know that His Word is living and active!

Write, recite and repeat. Repetition, repetition, repetition.

Another beautiful reason is that God is <u>omniscient </u>and our enemy is not.

Our God is all-powerful. He has no limits. This means when we read scripture or pray silently, God can hear us, He knows exactly what we are saying and conveying to Him. The enemy is not aware because he is not omniscient. Now, there are times the evil one does not need to know what our conversations are with our Lord and Savior. There are also times where we want the enemy to know exactly what we are saying and he can tremble away!

This is when quoting scripture and/or praying out loud is crucial. It is aimed at reminding the enemy that you have not forgotten to Whom you belong.

Omniscient ~ unlimited knowledge and awareness - all knowing.

Psalm 139:1-4

[1] O Lord, You have searched me and known me,

[2] You know my sitting down and my rising up;

You understand my thought afar off.

[3] You comprehend my path and my lying down,

And are acquainted with all my ways

[4] For there is not a word on my tongue,

But behold, O Lord, You know it altogether.

_____
_____
_____
_____
_____
_____
_____
_____

Hebrews 4:13

¹³And there is no creature hidden from His sight,

but all things are naked and open to the eyes of Him

to whom we must give account.

Psalm 147:4-5

⁴ He counts the number of stars;

He calls them all by name.

⁵ Great is our Lord, and mighty in power;

His understanding is infinite.

So far, we have covered many things ~ who exactly our God is, who you are in Him. Who the conniving enemy is and the confidence and boldness that the Lord has designed you to walk in. We have covered the fact that the Lord did not make a mistake about creating you and He has given you everything that you need to be prepared and armed where this enemy is concerned.

How do you feel knowing that you have been called to be both a witness and a warrior? This is serious business indeed.

What are your thoughts about where you are with your relationship with Jesus and are you ready to suit up and take care of business for the Kingdom and your family? Write out a prayer asking for God to guide you in this endeavor. Spend time praising Him and thanking Him for all He has given you and equipped you for.

_____

_____

_____

_____

_____

_____

_____

_____

_____

_____

_____

_____

_____

_____

_____

Week Five

~ Praying ~

"When asked, `What is more important:

Prayer or Reading the Bible?

I ask, `What is more important: Breathing in or Breathing out? `"

Charles Spurgeon

Imagine what it could mean for both, you and your families, if you began each day with premeditated purpose and solid erudition, using God's word to glean this erudition? You would be in a radically intentional mode with our Jesus and this my friends, means you would be a mighty force to be reckoned with where the evil one is concerned. Your prayer life would play a huge role in your position.

Praying is just as important as spending time in God's Word. Praying is not to be underestimated and should never be taken lightly. It is part of this serious business that you and I need to be about, it is also one of the sweetest times you can spend with your Lord.

I heard someone say that praying substitutes the situation from our own strength to God's. This is true when we are aligned with His will. There is always victory when we allow God at the helm instead of vying for that position ourselves.

This "sweet" prayer is also a mighty weapon. A weapon that can downright demolish strongholds.

2 Corinthians 10:3-4

3 For though we walk in the flesh, we do not war

according to the flesh·

4 For the weapons of our warfare are not carnal

but mighty in God for pulling down strongholds, ...

_____

_____

_____

_____

_____

Praying is precious time talking with our Lord. It is spending time with Him. It is calling on the name of Jesus and reminding the enemy who we belong to: telling the evil one to flee, to get behind you because it is the Lord Jesus who goes before you.

Deuteronomy 31:8

8 And the Lord, He is the One who goes before you.

He will be with you, He will not leave you nor forsake you;

do not fear nor be dismayed.

_____

_____

_____

_____

Matthew 16:23a

23aBut He turned and said to Peter, "Get behind Me, satan!"

_____

_____

_____

In the above scripture Jesus is actually speaking to Peter. This is a great reminder that sometimes, the people we know and even love can be a stumbling block for us. It is up to us if we allow them to be a hinderance or to nip things in the bud like Jesus did. (not that you want to look Aunt Sally in the eye and say get behind me satan. But I hope you understand what I'm saying here)

Our Lord wants us to call on Him. He wants us to chat with Him. Prayer does not have to be eloquent or long.

Our God knows every hair on our head and every hurt in our heart. There is not anything that we could say which would take Him by surprise. He not only knows our hearts but He knows that sometimes we just need to pour it out to Him. Sit and weep with Him, this lets down our walls and allows us to commune with Him and just lean in to Him. Letting go of the things that we don't need to hold on to while leaning in and soaking up more of our God.

Have you ever vented your feelings to a friend and felt so much better afterwards? This is exactly what the Lord is wanting us to do with Him. What if He became our first go-to when we had a problem before going to other people? There is a time for wise and Godly counsel but often we take to friends and other people the very thing we should be bringing directly to our Lord.

In 1 Samuel chapter 1, Hannah is praying. She understood who God was and she wept in anguish and poured her heart out to the Lord. She was so passionate that Eli, the high priest, thought her to be drunk.

When was the last time you prayed with passion and fervor?

I love how Hannah prayed in chapter 2 of 1 Samuel. There is no question that she knew and loved her Lord God Almighty.

1 Samuel 2:2

² No one is holy like the Lord,

For there is none besides You,

Nor is there any rock like our God

_____

_____

_____

_____

There are times we are in utter despair and need a good pouring out of the heart with our Lord and there are times when we give Him the praise for who He is. He wants our pouring out, our weeping, our bitterness, our praise and thanksgiving.

I recommend that you have a prayer journal, or journal period. I love to do this, but some don't. If you do then I highly recommend doing so. Journal about your prayers and spending time with Him. It is also a great tool to record things you are thankful for. Journal what you are praying for and throughout time go back and see how the Lord has been working. I recently ran across prayers I had written over twenty years ago and it was a mighty sweet thing to re-read them.

There are so many scriptures about praying but I love Jeremiah 33:3. This is one our children and grandchildren should know as a reminder that we can always call out to the Lord. Some people call this God's phone number.

Jeremiah 33:3

3 Call to Me, and I will answer you,

and show you great and mighty things,

which you do not know.

_____

_____

_____

_____

Matthew 18:19-20

19 Again I say to you that if two of you agree on earth

concerning anything that they ask,

it will be done for them by My Father in heaven.

20 For where two or three are gathered together in My name,

I am there in the midst of them.

_____

_____

_____

_____

Find a prayer partner if you don't already have one. For that matter find a couple of prayer warriors. I have heard it said that when you sit at the table of warriors, the conversation is different. I know this for a fact!

Praying with others is a beautiful thing, but we also need to be praying when we are alone. This was something that even Jesus did. He would get away from the crowd and pray, spending time with His Father in heaven.

Mark 1:35

35 Now in the morning, having risen a long while

before daylight, He went out and departed

to a solitary place; and there He prayed.

The intimacy we develop with regular one on one time with the Lord is mighty special. The more time we spend with Him, the more we will know His voice.

Ephesians 6:18a

18aPraying always...

Philippians 4:6-7

[6] Be anxious for nothing, but in everything by prayer

and supplication, with thanksgiving,

let your requests be made know to God

[7] and the peace of God, which surpasses all understanding

will guard your hearts and minds through Christ Jesus.

_____

_____

_____

_____

_____

_____

_____

_____

We should not even waste our energy being anxious and worrying, instead spending time boldly and with confidence at the throne of grace. I am aware this may be easier said than done. This is why we need to be bringing it to the Lord Jesus. But notice we should be thankful and definitely sharing in our prayers that we are thankful.

We teach our children to say thank you as early as a baby still on our hip. Anytime someone hands them something or blesses them with a compliment we ask our child to say "thank you". We are busy teaching them to be thankful to the giver and yet how often are we thanking our heavenly Father for all the good and beautiful things He has blessed us with, or the "hard" that He has seen us through.

James 1:17

Every good gift and every perfect gift is from above...

_____

_____

1 Thessalonians 5:16-18

[16] Rejoice always,

[17] Pray without ceasing,

[18] in everything give thanks;

for this is the will of God in Christ Jesus for you.

_____

_____

_____

Ephesians 5:20

[20] Giving thanks always for all things to God the Father

in the name of our Lord Jesus Christ

_____

_____

_____

Colossians 4:2

2 Continue earnestly in prayer,

being vigilant in it with thanksgiving

_____

_____

Psalm 95:2

2 Let us come before His presence with thanksgiving;

Let us shout joyfully to Him with psalms

_____

_____

Romans 12:12

12 Rejoicing in hope, patient in tribulation,

continuing steadfastly in prayer

_____

_____

_____

When we have seen horrific things and lived through the worst of the worst – this does not mean that you rejoice or give thanks for what happened. No – It means that we have the beautiful confidence of knowing that in spite of whatever the "ugly" was that has happened or is happening, that our Jesus can and will see us through. We don't have to like it one stinking bit, but what an incredible praise that- He will fill you with peace and allow you to withstand. Giving Him the glory and reminding the enemy Who we belong to.

Jesus is the perfect example of our need to pray.

John 17:9

⁹"I pray for them. I do not pray for the world but for

those whom You have given Me, for they are Yours.

_____

_____

_____

Luke 6:12

¹² Now it came to pass in those days that He went out to the

mountain to pray and continued all night in prayer to God.

_____

_____

_____

Have you ever been so distraught that you could not even pray? You wanted to but the words would not come? I have. The deep sobs take control and the words that you want to say seem to be absorbed by the sobs – I have beautiful news for you! The Holy Spirit intercedes on our behalf when we find ourselves too broken to utter words. How precious is this.

Romans 8:26-27

[26] Likewise the Spirit also helps in our weaknesses.

For we do not know what we should pray for as we ought,

but the Spirit Himself makes intercession for us with groanings which cannot be uttered.[27] Now He who searches the hearts

knows what the mind of the Spirit is,

because He makes intercession for the saints

according to the will of God.

_____

_____

_____

_____

_____

_____

_____

_____

Knowing the Holy Spirit intercedes is so very personal to me. I believe it is because in my walk with the Lord there have been times when I depended on this. I did not even have to be conscientious of the fact but in the midst of it all I could feel the peace raining down on me.

I hope you have been spending some sweet time in prayer with the Lord this week.

I also hope that you can feel your time in God's Word, with Him and in prayer evolving into something more beautiful than ever.

Write out a prayer asking the Lord to guide you in your time with Him, and seeking more of Him. Helping you to tune out distractions and tune more in to Him.

_____

_____

_____

_____

_____

_____

_____

_____

_____

_____

_____

_____

_____

_____

_____

_____

_____

_____

Week Six

~ Heed/ Obey ~

A whole lot of what we call "struggling"

is simply delayed obedience.

Elizabeth Elliot

As a child, I loved doing anything that my daddy was doing. I am very close to my daddy and definitely a daddy's girl. I stuck to him like glue. My childhood was tumultuous and my daddy was my rock. When I was next to him, all seemed right with the world.

My daddy taught me so many things growing up but what I loved the most was that he was just there and present. One of the many things he would take me to do was fishing. I believe my favorite part, other than just being with him, was stocking up on our fishing snacks. My daddy had an incredible sweet tooth and so did I. He never skimped on the snacks. So, snacks stocked and off we would go to fish.

The hardest part about all this fishing was that I had to be quiet and I had to keep my eye on the bobber. Being quiet was the biggest struggle. Keeping my eye on that bobber, that I could do. Yes, sometimes I would get distracted but I learned pretty quick that if my eye was on it, I would not miss my catch.

When we stay focused on our heavenly Father, we won't miss His blessing. We won't miss what He is showing us and the "so much more" that He has for us. When we are focused on Him, we may not be able to see beneath all that is going on, but rest assured, He is working.

Heed ~ means to pay careful attention to, take notice of.

Most of the time we do not always do this with scripture, God's Word. Especially with the verses we are familiar with. Familiarity leads to comfort and too much comfort can lead to a taking for granted, or complacency.

Have you ever found yourself zipping through a verse when saying it out loud. Saying it super-fast? However, how much more beautiful is His word when we read it or say like the incredibly powerful words they are, some even being poetic. Taking time to truly hear them and soak them up, meditating on them.

When we blow through God's Word to check off a "to-do" box, even when not realizing what we are doing, we aren't heeding His word.

We need to slow down, taking His word seriously and allowing it to fill us up. When we take His word seriously – we are taking Him seriously. He mentions giving His word heed, "more earnest heed" to be exact. If for no other reason, we should do this because, God said so. This is where our obedience comes in to action.

At the end of the day, we can hear and read His Word but if we put zero action behind it, then it won't mean diddly do.

Hebrews 2:1

1 Therefore we must give the more earnest heed

to the things we have heard,

lest we drift away.

_____

_____

_____

_____

We are to heed so we won't drift away. This is telling us to be intentional with the scriptures and to hang on to the Truth so we don't drift.

Drifting ~ this is what boats do when not firmly in place or on course – they drift. When we are intentional and diligent about God's Word, we become firmly rooted. Once rooted ~ we don't drift.

Colossians 2:6-7

⁶ As you therefore have received Christ Jesus the Lord,
so walk in Him, ⁷ rooted and built up in Him
and established in the faith, as you have been taught,
abounding in it with thanksgiving.

_____

_____

_____

_____

_____

_____

When our roots run deep, we won't be drifting.

Jeremiah 17: 7-8

⁷ Blessed is the man who trusts in the Lord, and whose hope
is the Lord ⁸ For he shall be like a tree planted
by the waters, which spreads out its roots by the river
and will not fear when heat comes; but its leaf
will be green, and will not be anxious in the year
of drought, nor will cease from yielding fruit.

_____

_____

_____

_____

_____

_____

_____

_____

I don't know about y'all but to me this is a beautiful thing ~ firmly rooted, established, abounding, no fear, truth knowing and still bearing fruit. Yes, I will take that, please and thank you!

I feel like "heed" goes hand in hand with abiding. We need to stop trying to medal in multitasking and be more purposeful with our time.

Trust me when I say that I do understand. When you have a house full of littles, life can get CrAzy. Shucks, one little baby can disrupt your usual routine, not to mention the husband, job, etc. I get it, which is why it takes intentionality and a premeditated purpose.

Sometimes we need to say the word "no". The people pleaser in me had a hard time with this and I had to learn this the hard way. When we have too many irons in the fire it is almost a guarantee that God is no longer our priority. He has slowly slipped down the list to, "I'll get to that/Him later" or I'll figure it out later.

John 15:1, 4

¹ I am the true vine, and My Father is the vinedresser.

⁴ Abide in Me, and I in you. As the branch

cannot bear fruit of itself, unless it abides in the vine,

neither can you, unless you abide in Me.

_____

_____

_____

_____

_____

Life gets tough and it is not for the faint of heart. We can't do this thing called life without Jesus. Our time in His Word and with Him, poured in and soaking Him up will never be regretted.

Proverbs 8:17

¹⁷ I love those who love Me,

and those who seek me diligently

will find me.

_____

_____

_____

_____

Notice the word diligently. <u>Diligently</u> – in a way that shows care and conscientiousness.

<u>Shachar</u> – this word, a Hebrew word for diligently is used 12 times throughout scripture. When we do this very thing, it perpetuates a beautiful cycle and we are definitely blessed.

We see this "diligently" again in Hebrews.

Hebrews 11:6

⁶ But without faith it is impossible to please Him,

for he who comes to God must believe that He is,

and that He is a rewarder of those who

diligently seek Him.

_____

_____

_____

_____

_____

_____

Psalm 63:1-8

[1] O God, You are my God;

Early will I seek You;

My soul thirsts for you;

My flesh longs for You

In a dry and thirsty land

Where there is no water.

[2] So I have looked for You in the sanctuary,

To see Your Power and Your glory,

[3] Because your Loving kindness is better

Than life

My lips shall praise You

[4] Thus I will bless You while I live;

I will lift up my hands in Your name.

[5] My soul shall be satisfied as with

marrow and fatness,

and my mouth shall praise You with joyful lips.

[6] When I remember You on my bed,

I meditate on You in the night watches.

[7] Because you have been my help,

Therefore in the shadow of Your wings

I will rejoice

[8] My soul follows close behind You;

Your right hand upholds me.

_____
_____
_____
_____
_____
_____
_____
_____
_____
_____
_____
_____
_____
_____
_____
_____
_____
_____
_____
_____
_____

How beautiful! I was only going to type in verse 1 but could not bring myself to stop. These verses are so precious! The psalmist, David, "thirsts & longs" for the Lord. He knows and has experienced the Lord's loving kindness and it is "better than life." He is so filled with worship for the Lord it is overflowing and he can't help but to raise his hands in praise to God.

Have you felt your worship for the Lord overflowing lately?

The more we seek Him, the more we love Him. The more we love Him, the more we want even more of Him. The Great I AM designed it this way. I also believe that when we don't take advantage of Him and all He has to offer to us by drawing near to Him, then we miss out on so much that He wants to freely give us.

Heed, abide and obey. When we heed God's Word we naturally want to abide with Him and the more we abide with Him the more we desire to be obedient. Our obedience honors God, therefore when we don't obey, it dishonors Him.

God always has His reasons for what He ask of us or calls us to. Our job is simply, heed, obey and of course, trust. When we do this, it only draws us in more intimately with the One who loves us the most.

Obey ~ comply with the command, direction or request: submit to the authority of.

Exodus 19:5

19Now therefore, if you will indeed obey My voice

and keep My covenant, then you shall be a special treasure

to Me above all people; for all the earth is Mine.

_____

_____

_____

It's really plain and simple. We can't serve two masters. If we are not honoring, serving and obeying Christ Jesus our Lord then we are making the enemy very happy.

Matthew 6:24

24No one can serve two masters; for either he will

hate the one and love the other, or else he will be loyal to

the one and despise the other.

_____

_____

_____

The Lord doesn't want us to be lukewarm. Look back in the beginning of the book where I posted about this -I posted **Revelation 3:15-16**.

At the end of the day, we can hear and read His Word but if we put zero action behind it, then it won't mean squat. We are called to do more than just hear/read His Word. We are only fooling ourselves if we listen to the Pastor on Sunday and live for ourselves during the week.

James 1:22

²²But be doers of the word, and not hearers only,

deceiving yourselves.

_____

_____

_____

Choose this day Whom you will serve. Put away what hinders you.

Joshua 24:14 &15b

¹⁴ᵃNow, therefore, fear the Lord, serve Him in sincerity

and in truth… Put away the gods your father's served…

¹⁵ᵇ But as for me and my house,

we will serve the Lord

_____

_____

_____

_____

_____

We have not been called to straddle the fence. We have been called by a Holy God, to be about some serious business for His kingdom.

God has called us to be witnesses and warriors for the kingdom, our families and in our own backyard – for each of you who claim the role "Christ Follower":

The *College Age* – you are called to be a light, an example – set apart.

The *Mama's* out there raising littles. Those littles you are raising, they are future Kingdom workers and builders and your role is priceless. The hand that rocks the cradle is a powerful thing, use it wisely.

The *Grandma's and Nana's,* - you are extending your legacy of Kingdom building even to the "grand" generation and I promise you that your children are still watching, no matter how grown they are.

The *Wife* – you are making an impact with your husband. **Proverbs 31:23** *"Her husband is known in the gates...*   You have great sway and an incredible influence with your husband, use it wisely.

So, while you are busy raising future Kingdom Builders, being a care giver, still rocking a career, making it through that next chemo treatment ~The King Himself is busy molding you into a mighty woman, handpicked and chosen by the Great I AM, who understands her position on the spiritual battlefield.

At the end of the day, or in the middle of the mayhem ~ remember Who you belong to, square your shoulders or hit your knees; but, act like the woman with premeditated purpose who is about her Father's business. After all, we serve an **Ephesians 3:20** God.

Suit up ladies, allow the armor of God to be a part of your daily life ~ there's a spiritual war going on, assume your position on this battlefield of life, standing firm on Who you belong to. The legacy you leave is for eternity. God handpicked you. He created you to be capable with His strength.

You were created on Purpose ~ with a Purpose ~ for His Purpose!

My prayer for you is *Colossians 1:10-14*

Colossians 1:10-14

¹⁰ that you may walk worthy of the Lord, fully pleasing Him,

being fruitful in every good work and increasing

in the knowledge of God; ¹¹ strengthened with all might,

according to His glorious power, for all patience

and longsuffering with joy; ¹² giving thanks to the Father

who has qualified us to be partakers of the inheritance

of the saints in the light. ¹³ He has delivered us from

the power of darkness and conveyed us into the kingdom

of the Son of His love, [14] in whom we have redemption

through His blood, the forgiveness of sins.

Write out a prayer, praising and thanking Him and asking God to strengthen your foundation in Him and your faith. Helping you to be deeply rooted with a heart willing to fully surrender in obedience to Him.

_____
_____
_____
_____
_____
_____
_____
_____
_____
_____
_____
_____

I pray that you have been blessed and have fallen deeper in love with your Jesus and His Word in a fresh new way. I have added some additional pages for thoughts, prayers and notes.

_____
_____
_____
_____
_____
_____
_____
_____
_____
_____
_____
_____
_____
_____
_____
_____
_____
_____
_____
_____
_____
_____

_____
_____
_____
_____
_____
_____
_____
_____
_____
_____
_____
_____
_____
_____
_____
_____
_____
_____
_____
_____
_____
_____
_____
_____
_____
_____
_____
_____
_____
_____

Premeditated Purpose

Premeditated Purpose

129

Other Books by Toni Cowart

All available on *AMAZON*

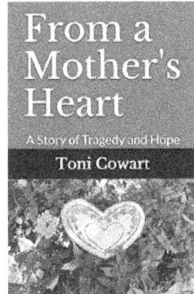

From a Mother's Heart
A Story of Tragedy and Hope
Toni Cowart

Now What ??
Toni Cowart

The Chipmunk, the Bird and the Slithering Slimies
Toni Cowart

The Bird, The Raccoon and The Skunk without a Stripe
Toni Cowart

Premeditated Purpose

www.ingramcontent.com/pod-product-compliance
Lightning Source LLC
Chambersburg PA
CBHW052342100426
42736CB00047B/3409